Prospecting & Small Scale Mining 1- The Centrifuge

Tim Johnson
Copyright © 2019 Tim Johnson

ISBN: 9781708479312

DEDICATION

I'd like to dedicate this, my latest foray into the depravity of the written word, to Alex and John Ray, a couple of Canuckelheads that allowed me to run their centrifuges for a bit. The experiences at their little mine were invaluable to learning the ins and outs of centrifuge design and operation. While the ones I have built to date are a far cry from those commercialized masterpieces, they are what took me down the path into that particular rabbit hole and my later work will get better.

CONTENTS

ACKNOWLEDGMENTS

To my father, Ted Johnson. To my grandfather, Floyd Johnson. They got me started in prospecting. Infected me with Gold Fever at an early age. To the countless books and prospecting partners who's help proved invaluable as well as people like Dave Stewart, who's wealth of old time local information kept me finding gold at a time when not finding it meant starvation for me and those that depended on me. To Mike Finley, who bought so much of my gold back then. Ive outlived so many of them but their help got me where I am today. To Jennifer, for believing in me.......

1

GOLD FEVER

I have been involved with mining and prospecting most of my life. The tools and techniques that got me started had to be learned from books, pictures and stories and then turned into practical knowledge by applying those things to the real world. I generally had to build my own equipment since I could not afford to buy anything beyond the most basic things like gold pans and shovels. I built fairly advanced equipment from pictures in magazines, copied the latest and greatest from the Keene Engineering catalog. It didn't matter to me, I would steal ideas from anyone! I would build out of wood, steel and aluminum. I learned carpentry because of prospecting, I needed the skills. I also learned to weld because I needed the skill to make the tools that I needed. I would get old highway signs from the road department and use them to build equipment. I once paid kids in metal shop at the high school to build me a custom sluice box as I was too young to enter their program. How did I get started? It happened at a very young age. My dad and my grandfather infected me with gold fever at the tender age of six or seven years. We were camping in Northern California on the Siskiyou Fork of the Smith River. 1973 I think. My grandfather was always out exploring by himself and this one day he came back to camp very excited about a spot that he had located and took a sample from. A place that he said just smelled of a rich gold deposit. He had brought a small paper bag of dirt back with him and had my dad get me from the tent where I was reading about mountain men, miners and outlaws in some old west style magazine. Yes, I was a book worm even back then and addicted to that bygone era. Just as soon as I learned to read, I read everything i could. They insisted that I be the one to pan the sample as they were just too darned excited and might loose the gold. I smelled a rat right off and gave them the third degree about where the dirt came from, why they wanted someone who had never panned before to do it when they were both experienced and how he just happened to have a paper bag with him on the hike to put the dirt in. Those two had an answer for everything. I wasn't buying it though but kept my suspicions to myself. I was just happy to be included in some pretty adult stuff for once. They did bribe me by saying I could shoot the .22 rifle when we were done there. Satisfied for the moment, I took that huge steel gold pan and dumped the bag of dirt into it. My grandmother had showed up to watch and confiscated the paper bag, which she then neatly folded for reuse. People that lived through the depression didn't waste ANYTHING that could be reused. I submerged the pan in the back eddy of the river where we had camped and started swirling it the way I had seen my elders and how I had read that it was done. I picked out the bigger rocks and kept working it slowly and carefully, washing out the clays and picking out rocks as they appeared on the back side of the pan. I then started the side to side shaking and washing the lighter gravel out, picking oversized as needed. Pretty much everyone standing in awe as I was doing the first pan of my life somewhat professionally without any instruction. It took me a good ten minutes to get it down to the black sands and about that time, yellow was shining through. I was pretty excited when I finished and exposed what had to be about a million dollars in gold out of one pan. One look at their faces told me the truth. It wasn't real. It sure looked real. Well, it seems that they conspired for quite some time on this prank and my dad had gone to the mechanic and welder that worked for him at the fish company he managed in Crescent City and got him to melt up some nuggets out of brass brazing rod in support of the conspiracy. The long and short of it was from that moment on, prospecting has been in my blood. I've found quite a bit of gold over the years and worked for many mines, both small and large and I still prefer the finding to the mining.

I decided that I should pass on a bit of my knowledge that might help some of the old hands and newcomers alike. This is intended to be a series of books. It's probably going to take twenty books or more to cover the information that I would like to pass along. At least this self publishing medium will allow me to keep the cost down just as low as I can to help my fellow miners learn and find gold. Either as a hobby or as a career, mining is necessary for our society to survive and prosper. Remember; if it isn't grown, it has be be mined. This series will cover subjects from prospecting techniques to equipment choices and how to build needed equipment from scratch. I'm even planning to take a trip into lapidary work. Precious and semi precious stones and jewelry making are part of the industry too. I've prospected a lot of different country and I've extracted gold where others have failed. I taught myself the lab skills to do my own assays for gold and silver as well. I've mined placers, and I have mined hard rock. This stuff is going to come at you one topic at a time in no particular order. I hope you manage to take something from this that you can use. God only knows where I would be today had this all be available to me from the get go!

2

THE CENTRIFUGE

The centrifuge is relatively new in the mining and prospecting world. At least in comparison to most other mining technologies in use. The concept uses the benefits of the centrifugal force of a spinning object to make the gravity separation of minerals easier. At 400 "G's", or gravities, the mass of a particle is extremely magnified. This gravity enhancement tends to widen the specific gravity spread between minerals and make the concentration of smaller target particles formerly lost in process, possible. This process makes all other concentration methods obsolete. Not an exaggeration. FACT. Sluices, tables, pan type concentrators, spiral wheels and spirals, all obsolete. These devices can catch particles in the three micron range for non fluid bed machines and ten times that for fluid beds. Fluid bed concentrators use water pressurized from behind the cone that enters the riffles through tiny holes drilled through. This water keeps the material the riffles somewhat fluid so it can uptake heavy particles more quickly than the other type. The tradeoff is a lower efficiency of particle size concentrated. Classification of material is extremely important for these enhanced gravity units. Water flow that can flush a less dense particle of 3 millimeters would also flush gold particles many times smaller, costing you money. In the mining world, we have a few basic types of centrifugal concentrators. The most important to us are the batch or cementation type and the continuous concentrator. The are many differences between brands within the same basic type as well. Enhancements that make them more suited for one type of processing over another. Sometimes the differences are more of a marketing ploy rather than an enhancement. The slurry of water and solids enters the concentrator at the bottom center of the cone or tube and travels up the wall of the spinning device as a film, depositing its heavier constituents in riffles that are cast or machined around it inside surface. The continuous concentrators generally have a limited water outflow at the first riffle of its cone or tube. This slight outlet flow allows a percentage of the heaviest minerals to exit as an enriched slurry. The rest of the slurry travels up and out of the concentrator, leaving heavier particles in the riffles along the way as a normal cementation concentrator would. The enriched slurry would go to another machine for further enrichment or directly to another process, such as leaching. The mineral concentrating centrifuge is enormously complex and expensive. Does it have to be? No. One of the earliest useful and commercially successful centrifuges was a cream separator for dairies and home use. Very simple and many were hand operated via cranks and gears. While that seems a bit under powered for our use as a mineral concentrator, perhaps something just a bit more complex yet lacking all the electronics and solenoid operated valves, etc. of the more complex units would serve the small miner and prospector better. I do know a bit about them as I ran concentrators at mines that I've worked for. One mine used a 48 inch Knelson centrifuge to concentrate the slurry from its placer operations. It was a batch concentrator that flushed twice a day, leaving about 150 pounds of concentrate from both flushes. This concentrate needed to be reconcentrated to make it suitable for panning by hand. While some people have used more simple low tech items to accomplish this, using the same technology is important because when the advanced unit can concentrate gold to 3 microns, you wouldn't want to waste that gold by flushing it through a sluice box that can't catch a 100 micron piece, let alone gold in the single digits on the micron scale. I used another Knelson, a 7.5 inch unit. Then, I hand panned to clean it up and have it ready to melt, sometimes panning as much as 10 pounds a day. Yes. Ten pounds. Of gold. A day. This isn't to say that the other equipment obsoleted by the centrifuge isn't still useful. I use a sluice as a backup to the centrifuge to give a visual indicator of what's happening inside the box of the centrifuge. For testing and remote work where size really does matter, the centrifuge can't compete.

3

BUILDING A CENTRIFUGE

Your centrifuge can be as small or large and as simple or as complex as you want it to be. The smaller, lab sized concentrator is limited to a couple hundred pounds of material an hour and might be best used as a test tool or reconcentrator but is also great when used for sampling multiple areas quickly in the field. The lab sized unit will have a three or four inch cone. Little power is required to spin these, a 1/4 horsepower motor being more than enough. A six to eight inch cone can handle more throughput and may get you over the hump in the ton per hour range. This guide is aimed at the beginner looking to build his first machine so there is no reason to be concerned with units bigger than those mentioned at this time, within the pages of this book. Power can come from an electric motor, gas engine or even water or steam power assuming you can gear or pulley up to the RPM needed. What RPM is needed? It depends in large part to the particle size of gold that you have in you ore. Higher RPM equals higher G forces exerted. A gas engine allows you to use the throttle, or governor control, to control RPM. Direct drive, without the headache of pulleys and belts becomes possible since most engines govern at 3,600 RPM at their top end. With a four inch cone, 3,000 RPM will apply nearly 400 G's to the top of the cone, decreasing linearly to the center, or bottom of the cone. I wont say that 400 G's is the highest that you will need to separate your particular ore but it is a good high end target for your gearing for a test machine. Its far easier to reduce RPM with a motor control than it is to get higher than rated speed from a motor. Ideally, some control should be present in your design to fine tune the machine for the ore being run. The RPM and resulting G's must be within the mechanical capabilities of your spun parts. You don't want things exploding, sending shrapnel out that could easily kill or maim. Assuming you wish to run your cone or tube inverted or with the open end up, your motor and drive system will have to be built to accommodate this. They will work on the horizontal though if you can feed it water and muck in this position. This position does completely away with the issues of sealing the water flow away from the bottom bearing. As for the bottom bearing, at least on manufacturer uses the bearing and shaft from the deck of a riding lawnmower. This tower shaped bearing keeps the water flooding the bottom of the unit from attacking the bearing or draining from the unit when the bearing assembly is sealed with silicone to prevent this. A skirt can extend down from the cone to help keep slurry flung off the cone at speed from getting to the bearing. So, we need to account for drive motive power available, shafts and pulleys needed and support bearings. The job must be planned out in detail considering what you have to work with, including money. If the drive components will break the bank, go horizontal and work through design difficulties with plastic pipe, plywood, dimensional lumber and silicone caulking. Or just use an old drill press. Think about it; it has a fairly powerful motor, many speeds from a few hundred RPM to over 3,000 (usually). While you could leave it in its upright position and drive it from above, it's an easy matter to flip it inverted, cut the support tube down and run it that way. So, the hundreds of dollars in parts I was looking for just became a $100 five speed drill press from Harbor Tools? Yup, plenty of speed and power to run a four inch cone lab machine. A bigger drill press would be needed to run bigger cones but is certainly feasible. For field use, a small generator would be needed. Not a bad idea to go electric anyway so cheap pool pumps can be employed to recirculate your water. Well, this is how I built my first one…..

4

THE DESIGN

I started by obtaining a rubber centrifuge cone from a source that I found in Australia. I had looked high and low trying to find available used or new spares for existing machines and talked to the one manufacturer in the states that would talk to me. He really wasn't interested in selling me anything other than a new machine. His prices weren't that bad at less than $1500 delivered from Indiana. But, I had it in mind to build one to process my ore with and that's what I planned to do. I really wanted one on the order of the Knelson 7.5 inch model that I ran at one of my jobs but the cones in that size range were over $100 from that land down under. It wasn't that that was a lot of money but when you aren't sure of quality or suitability, it's best to tread lightly. They had a four inch size that promised to be delivered in three or four weeks for around $35, right off eBay. I decided to try that. When I received it, I was a little underwhelmed as it was just a light piece of neoprene rubber. But, since it was intended to be an insert for a machined cone, it likely didn't need to be very strong. I don't have the capabilities to make a cone from bar stock without it turning into a very expensive project, so I decided to see just how it would work suspended in mid air from a rim pinching it in place. So, in the interest of testing, I got a 3/4" grade eight bolt and turned a 1/2" shank on it to chuck into my big drill press. I had in mind to spin it at speeds to 3,000 RPM so I figured that if it could survive that without ripping apart or deforming until the riffles cast into it weren't functional, I should have something that could work. I found a four inch pipe nipple was a perfect fit for the cone, internally. I found a three inch cap that had a similar outside diameter to the nipple and after machining the nipple to length, taking into account the length needed for the cone to nest inside and the head of the bolt that I would use as a shaft, I welded the two together in the lathe to ensure it was as true as I could make it and thus, somewhat free from wobble. I hoped.

My boss at work has a CNC plasma cutter so I asked him it make two washers from 16 gauge steel scraps that could be used to pinch the cone in place. I first drilled holes through both washers to mach the cast holes in the cone and then welded one ring to the cup, then welding one inch sections of all thread rod to act as studs. I drilled through the pipe cap end slightly undersized and then finished the job with the boring bar until the 3/4" shaft I had made was a tight slip fit. Then I lathe welded it in place as well. I bolted it all together and installed the shaft in my drill press. I started spinning it in the 750 RPM range and while it was obviously at least a bit out of balance, it was doing ok. I spun it up in RPM incrementally until I had exceeded 3,000 RPM and seeing no obvious signs of failure, considered the test successful. I was trying to figure out how I wanted to build the new support tube and it came to me that if I had a more appropriately sized drill press, I could easily use that as my power unit, especially if I inverted it. After I had my little revelation about the drill press, I pulled an old one out of the junk pile at work and checked it out. It looked like that it had been thrown away because the belt failed. A trip to the NAPA store would solve that little issue. My bosses at the mine got involved at that point as they were working up an ore test that required a centrifuge of the lab sized variety to decide if they wanted to pay for a commercial unit and, just like that, I was building my centrifuge for them. So, I was going to get paid by the hour to test the theories involved so that I could better build a better one for myself? I sure as hell didn't see anything wrong with that theory at all. I took all of the parts home and worked through the weekend and had something to test by Monday. If I build another that size, I will use a piece of 4" pipe of 1/4" wall, a round plate purchased off eBay and drilled to accept a 3/4" weld in sprocket hub. I'll weld it all together in the lathe and will have a better rotating assembly. I'll use the mentioned lawn mower bearing assembly, and a pillow block or flanged bearing for extra support below and drive it all with pulleys and belt from a vertical shaft engine.

5

BUILDING IT

I had a few parts, and a rough idea of what i wanted so I visited my lumber pile to verify that I had enough lumber to get somewhere with the prototype. I had plenty of steel tube in round and square as well as galvanized and stainless sheet metal but wanted to use wood for the prototype. It's so much easier to undo mistakes or change direction. I had thought about making it with a round housing like all the commercial ones and decided that a long narrow housing might allow heavies missed by the cone to be seen as they settled on the bottom. This might aid in deciding the water flow and solid capacity of the unit. Had I gone for that idea, a plastic or steel bucket could have served for the housing. I used a piece of scrap 1/2 plywood left over from my magnetic separator build for the base. It just so happened to be almost the same footprint as that little drill press. I added a pair of 2X4's longitudinally to the bottom for stiffness and to provide mounting for the plywood sides. I then removed the base from and cut down the hight of the drill press. I also added a spacer 2X4 to the base where it would mount, so the drill press spindle and chuck would be properly placed. I marked and drilled for the mounting foot of the drill press in the base and drilled the through hole for the drive shaft. I assembled the drill to the base and installed the centrifuge cup so it could be tested. I had preset the belt and step pulley's for 3,000 RPM as that would be the most likely working speed of the unit. It ran pretty good, only a slight vibration and it spun up quickly so I suspected that this smaller drill press had more than enough power to do the job. I added four 2X4 legs, leaving them tall enough to support a screening or feed deck should I need one. I glued a section cut from a water filter housing to the base to help keep water from running out and onto the drill press. I cut sides, deciding to screw them to the legs from inside to simplify mounting and put the ends pieces in place, leaving an outlet gap of an inch so that most of the water flung off the top of the cone would be retained within and only allowed to exit the narrow opening at the bottom. Everything was sealed with plenty of silicone. I measured and cut a lid, using a 2X2 mounted at each end to keep it centered. I drilled a hole for the feed tube and then assembled 4"X1" PVC reducer as the feed bowl with pipe fittings and tube extending down into the cup to feed within 1/2" of the bottom of the cone. Plenty of silicone was used to seal and glue parts in their proper position. It was now done and ready for testing. Improvements for the next one this size would be aluminum sides, top, floor and ends. Most likely diamond plate. I'll probably keep the wood framing just to keep things simple.

6

THE TEST

Monday morning I loaded my little atom smasher, as it had been christened, into the back of my little Suzuki Vitara and headed for work. I made the machine so the legs at the outlet end could sit in the tails container with the other two legs propped level. After I turned it on, I noticed that the drill press bearing was a little loose, giving the cup a bit of wobble. I had decided to run it at a slight angle to help it flush tales and it turned out after blocking it up that way, the the gyro effect caused enough side thrust to cancel the wobble. A spinning object aways tries to be perpendicular to gravity. I installed a water flow meter on the inlet hose, setting the flow to indicate 5 gallons per minute (GPM). I turned it on and found that everything seemed happy, so I started feeding it 28 mesh screened ore, pre weighed at 25 lbs. I tried to keep it fed at a steady pace and was done in about 15 minutes. I turned the water flow off first, then turned off the centrifuge. I opened it up to look and saw a bit of black sand on the floor (my target mineral) and the cup's riffles were completely full of very heavy and black concentrates. The dry weight of the cons from the cleanout was 65 grams. Hardly a production tool but for getting samples to prove process, it was great. I then experimented over the next few hours with different pre measure weights and water flows but went back to the 25lbs over 15 minutes with 5 GPM as it gave a quality concentrate even though some of the sulfides I was after were lost. The assays showed that it was a success. This tool is fully capable of delivering over a kilo of cons per day with just one guy running it. I just could not do that with the concentrate table I had been running previously. This was enough to keep our lab rats very happy for the immediate future. This little tool went into production mode for the next month supplying cons for the lab and outside testing. I did add longitudinal 2X2 braces to the lid as it tended to warp when wet. Improvements: I also built a feed table for the top to aid in wetting the material before it entered the cone. Now its time to start working on the next one. Something that can approach a ton an hour of production for pilot testing....

7

THE NEXT BUILD

Since it was now time for a larger machine with a higher capacity to hold concentrates, and thus have more run time between clean outs, I started looking into possibilities. None of the builders of the darned things were interested in selling parts. Even when I explained that I needed to build the machine as a test bed so it could be changed as needed and quickly. It's a unique and complex ore and a cookie cutter machine wasn't going to make the grade. Or, at least it was highly unlikely that a machine built for gold concentration would be useful for the type of ore we were processing. One guy got really bent when I told him I was interested in buying his machine for its parts so I could rebuild it how we needed it. It was an expensive way to go but at the point we were at, it would have been the right thing for us. He even recalled emails that had been sent giving operational details! I didn't even know that was a thing. He absolutely wasn't interested in our business if we were going to modify his machine in any way. After more research, I found a marine plastics manufacturer that had molds for the cones and could supply small runs of parts. This made me think that other plastics manufacturers could likely do the same thing. If the manufacturer owns the molds, they can make the parts for anyone. But, since I was most interested in a batch machine that had really large and deep riffles, it was unlikely that these parts would fit our needs. Besides, there is liable to be a huge time issue here. Small runs of parts can be expensive and might very well result in quite a lead time. Perhaps that is an avenue to be explored when I am looking for more generic parts to build one for conventional prospecting or reconcentrating but I had been given an unrealistic set of goals because of the nature of this ore and I didn't think anything "generic" could work. I wanted it to run horizontally, direct mounted to a crankshaft or motor, be about 8-10 inches in diameter and cleanup without a teardown. The construction of feed tubes and providing a method of flushing the concentrates out of the unit seemed that it would make it needlessly complicated. I'm sure I can do it that way but for now, I wanted something I could make from what I had either on hand or close at hand with as little machining as possible……

8
BUILDING IT. AGAIN…..

Tube centrifuges were the direction I had been thinking about for a bigger machine, one capable of running about 1000 pounds per hour and to accumulate enough concentrates to meet the needs for the sulfide, oxide, etc deposit. The tests we need to run on these ores demand large amounts of concentrates with predictable quality. Our concentrator "cone" needed to have very deep riffles to allow the machine to run a certain amount of material over a short period of time to allow the proper enrichment ratio that we were looking for, yet produce enough pounds, or kilograms of product for the required tests. The design chosen would be a simple tube, six inches in diameter and six inches tall, with ring riffles welded into the tube to allow the material to concentrate inside the circumference of the tube. For someone needing to just concentrate gold, an insert of the type used in the previous design could be used. Obtain or make the insert first so it's holder, the drum, can be sized appropriately. From my research, many tube concentrators or centrifugal filters run horizontally but this ones needs to be run vertically for feeding and waste flush. There would be a drive hub welded into it and plugs in the bottom to allow cleaning. I wanted the self cleaning action of the tapered cone style, so I had the washers cut with progressively larger inside diameters to give the inside of the tube a cone shape, wider at the top. I had the cones cut by CNC out of material that was a bit light for welding with my MIG, but I managed to get it done, sealing the inside with silicone RTV would ensure no leakage of concentrates from the riffle grooves. Another possibility would be to make the rings and spacers out of plastic and using plastic cement to glue the parts together as they are laid into the part, sealing with silicone RTV to keep the gold out of cracks and crevices. I machined a center hole in a round flat plate to accept a machined hub with a 3/4 inch bore. I ordered the plate and hub off eBay. After cutting the pipe to length, welding in the riffles from the center out from each end, I welded on the plate and drive hub. Then I inverted it in my drill press and drilled and tapped holes in the bottom for pipe plugs to facilitate rinsing out of concentrates after a material run. I built the rest of the machine out of 3/4 ply, 2X4 lumber and star drive screws. I built it to taper towards a narrow exit, with a wide opening in the rear, accessible from the top, to place a pan under the bowl of the centrifuge to facilitate cleanup between runs. The shaft extends through the bowl but doesn't exit the bottom, The bottom bearing is bolted to the bottom of the unit and the shaft drives from the top which prevents the need for seals and such down below. The top and bottom bearings are flanged units. The 1.5 HP motor bolts on the side, pulley's to set the maximum speed needed with a variable frequency motor controller installed to control the RPM between the minimum and maximum. The larger machine is all but finished at this time but it's not going to be ready to run before this book hits the publisher. It will give you plenty of food for thought in your own construction though.

9

OPERATION OF THE CENTRIFUGE

Using centrifuges for gold mining is quite simple. The larger operation I worked at that used the technology used a 48 inch Knelson as the primary. They screened to 1/8 inch, with the sub 1/8 going through the concentrator and the 1/8 to 3/4 material going through a conventional sluice box. This was to catch nugget gold. The plus 3/4 was sent out the belts to the waste as it had been determined that very little gold existed in the deposit that would be lost in this fashion. The 48 inch concentrator would flush its concentrate twice daily. It is imperative that your feed be classified. the finer the better, as long as you aren't screening off gold. A nugget sluice for these screened materials is a good idea so values aren't lost. I would pick the cons up and then reconcentrate on the smaller 7.5 inch Knelson machine in the gold lab. I use a small aluminum sluice box at the outlet to alert me when the centrifuge is plugged up with gold. In the beginning I would pan its contents, now I just add it to the tails to rerun. I would run these cons and try to plug the machine with gold, enriching the concentrate in the machine as much as possible, saving the waste in buckets for reworking. Rich cons have to be run slow to allow the gold time to penetrate into the cone to be kept rather than washed out. It was my goal to get at least 12 ounces of gold per 14 inch pan as that was my most efficient sweet spot. Yes, that is a Troy pound of gold. Per pan. Sometimes I would get closer to two troy pounds and would have to use a 17 inch pan for final cleanup. I had days that I panned 3 pounds plus at once in the large pan. I would rerun cons until I had squeezed all the gold out of them. If the last cone of the run wasn't rich enough, I saved it to run with the next cleanup so as to make the most efficient use of my time. When you start a centrifuge, spin the centrifuge up to speed first. Then turn on your process water and set the pressure or flow of back pressure water for the floating bed if the device uses that feature. When you shut down the centrifuge, turn off the back pressure water, if used, then the process water and then turn off the centrifuge and allow it to spin down to a stop.

10

PANNING AND CLEANING THE GOLD

When panning, I separate out the magnetic black sands with one of those "gold magnets". Usually, a gold magnet is a magnet incased in a plastic or metal housing with a button or lever to raise and lower the magnet inside. They can be purchased on-line and in many outdoor stores that cater to the prospectors. I've used magnets held in the hand or even magnets placed inside a plastic freezer bag too. I usually put about 1/4 to 1/3 of a pan of rich material in the pan and then I pan until the magnetics become an issue. Sometimes this happens right away, causing gold loss, and I then use the magnet to either put the magnetics in the back of the pan or another pan filled with water where i will shake down and try to separate as much of the gold caught in the magnetic flux as I can before transferring them to a separate bucket. I do this several times in the process., sometime separating the magnetics from pan to pan to pan to get the best split of magnetics from non magnetics and to save as much gold as possible. The process works much better with water well over the magnetics you are trying to separate. When I have half a bucket or so of those nasty black magnetics, I add them to another cleanup run in the centrifuge to get back the gold trapped in them. Do not allow them to sit around wet or they will rust into a solid block on you. The only fix for that is impact milling. I'll publish a guide to making that tool in a later book. long term storage of black sands should include drying of them within a few days of their collection. Dried magnetic concentrates can be separated with a mechanical magnetic separator as well. Also to come in a later book… I also don't worry too much about gold losses into my panning tub as just as soon as its full or at some convenient point, I put those back through the centrifuge to get another crack at the gold I lost panning. Some products that are frequently found in concentrates like barite are an issue but I pan them to the far side of my pan, horizontally, and scrape them out from there to minimize my gold loss. I also use my off hand thumb to scrape lighter material off the edge of the pan so I'm not using so much hydraulic force that might carry gold with it. It also makes me feel better about sweeping gold into my tub this way rather than having the water wash it in. Don't sweat the loss as you are going to get it back next run anyway. Once the gold is as clean as is possible without spending too much time picking stuff out and shaking, adding soap again and again, I screen to about 20 mesh. If you did it right, the plus twenty fraction will be 100 percent clean gold. I then wash the minus fraction once more before drying. It's likely still 30 percent dross at that point but don't sweat it. I like to use stainless salad bowls on a hot plate for drying. It helps to crimp the rim so steam can escape when a steel gold pan is placed over it to contain splatter. tis a thing. You don't want your gold sent against the ceiling so cover it! Once it is dry, pour it back and fourth between two containers with a third container to accept waste. you will be able to clean it better this way dry. Keep it up until you have it as clean as you want and then pan/ dry the waste. It does take some practice but you can get large volumes of fine gold to 90 percent this way and that is more than clean enough to melt. Never dry gold in an environment that isn't well ventilated and preferably under a fume hood. Mercury can end up in the air this way, not to mention lead and other heavy metals and they can all poison you. If you plan to melt and pour your gold, you will need a furnace. Small amounts can be melted and poured with a torch. There will be shrinkage as some gold will go into the flux (pulverize and process the glass to get it back) and the lead, quartz and other minerals will be partly or completely removed from the gold during this step. I use electric ovens for my gold processing and assay work. I have used small LPG powered top loaders for melts before and they work well. Plans and instruction guides are available on the internet, videos on YouTube as well. Flux will be needed, most likely a straight borax product will be enough as long as your gold is clean enough. Anhydrous borax is preferred, but this is usually only available at suppliers that cater to assayers. The 20 mule team borax available at the grocery store can be used if you take into account the water weight and adjust your formula accordingly. The are flux recipes out there that all profess to be the best for any melt, smelt or assay. Ive seen recipes that call for anhydrous borax, soda ash, sodium or potassium nitrate, carbon, flour or other chemicals. Many of these recipes are for the smelting of ores, rather than the melting of precious metal concentrates and as such, they usually cause problems with foaming and boil overs, losses of gold in the flux. Don't chose a complicated formula before you have even tried a simple flux. Ideally, you would test a small amount of the "ore" with fluxes in 30 or 40 gram clay crucibles, taking notes and numbering the crucibles, searching for the most optimal outcome. Without going into too much detail, a proper flux will make a nice smooth pour at gold melt temperatures with a flux that doesn't consume the clay crucible and is not overly viscous or thin. It will form a nice translucent glass upon cooling and separate from the precious metals readily. There should be very little gold or silver "shot" in the glass and there should not be a layer of "spiese" between the gold or silver and the flux which will often trap values and cost you money. I've covered the subjects here adequately I think and you should be able to take advantage of this technology to increase your production, make concentrate cleanup simpler and quicker, mine lower grade ores often discarded at a profit. Now, go get some gold!

1

2

3

4

5

6

7

8

9

10

11

12

13

14

15

16

17

18

19

20

21

22

23

24

25

26

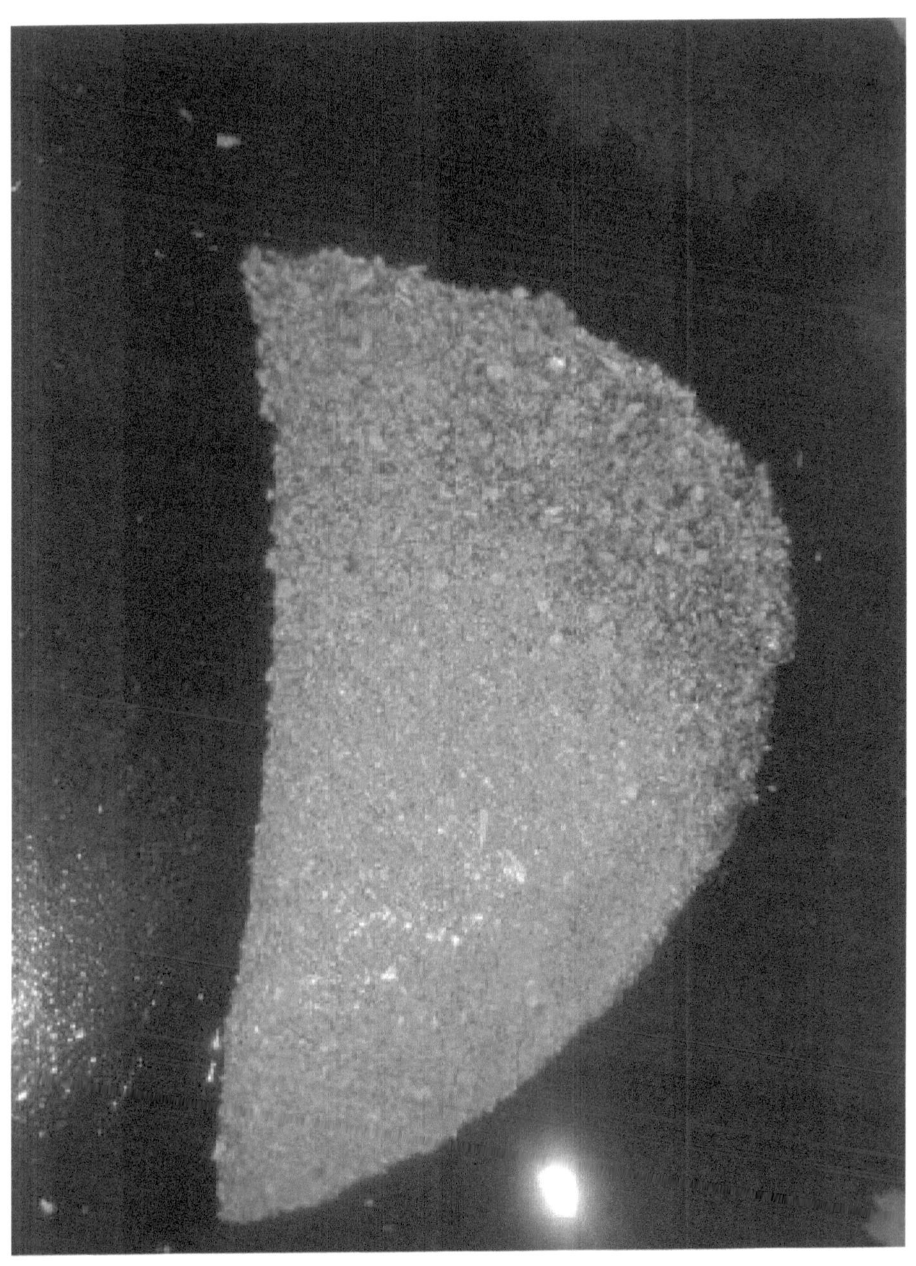

27

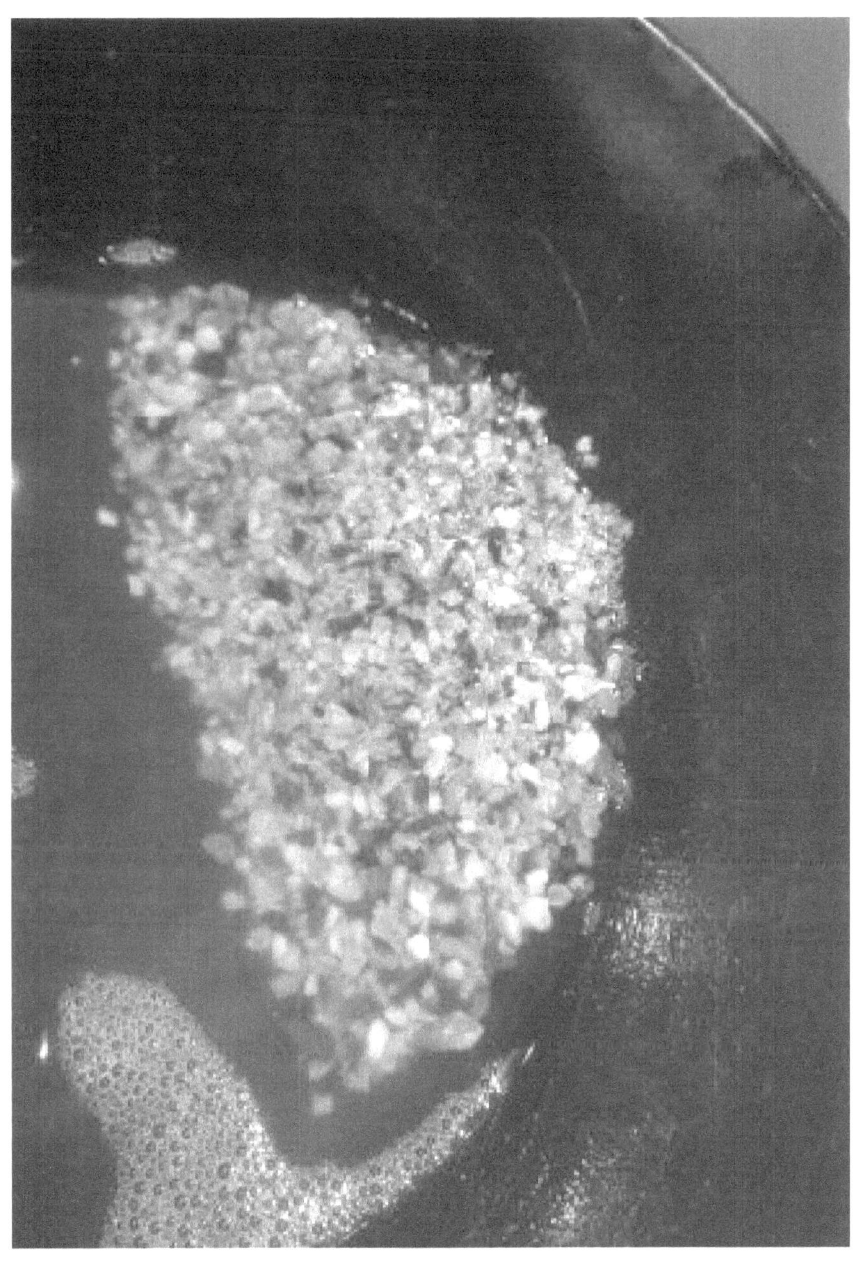

28

11
THE PICTURES

1- A view of the centrifuge after initial testing, as the wetting tray is being made and installed.

2- Another view, also showing the water flow meter used to set flow to proper limits. This type of meter shows total gallons, use a stop watch to calculate flow. The old style with a graduated tube and ball are very inexpensive and might be a better choice for the sake of simplicity.

3- The centrifuge power and drive unit, the drill press. I used a five speed China made unit. Salvaged from the junk pile. Bigger units can make bigger centrifuges.

4- Building the cup and drive shaft in the lathe. Note the step down shaft to allow it to chuck into the 1/2 inch drill press chuck. One four inch nipple, welded to a 3 inch cap and drilled for the 3/4 bolt I used to make the shaft. Bolts aren't as true and straight as shafting but it worked well enough,

5 View of the bottom of the drive unit during testing. Front legs are inside a steel 1/2 55 gallon drum. Rear legs are blocked up to match plus give a little tilt that helped cancel vibration. The blocking helps keep the belt chamber door closed. Safety first. Wouldn't want fingers to get into the belt…

6- Sowing the unit from the back during testing. The electrical control switch visible at bottom. Try to keep drips from this area and be sure to use GFI outlet for safety.

7 & 8- Feeding the machine with -28 mesh screened product. The proper feed rate is important.

the tailing exit through and into the 1/2 drum that its sitting in.

9- Front view of the unit during testing, not the rectangular opening that

10- Close side view of machine during test.

30

11- Another side view of the centrifuge during initial tests.

12- internal view of the rotating part of the centrifuge. The rubber insert is in place but not clearly visible. It is disassembled for cleaning by removing the four nuts visible here.

13- The feed hopper. A 3" X 1" reducer glued in place with clear silicone. The feed tube that releases the feed slurry just off the bottom of the cone was made up of steel nipples and PVC connectors all siliconed together. It's all that I could find at the time and it worked, so I didn't change it. The plywood top tended to warp so it was improved with 2X2 stiffeners later.

14- The CNC plasma cut rings welded into pipe to make the next centrifuge.

15- The 6 inch pipe, cut at 6 inches length used to make the larger cup for the next centrifuge.

16- The new cup with the end welded on and spinning between centers for cleanup of welds.

17- The drive hub welded into the new cup and ready for some lathe work to clean those ugly welds up.

18- The new cup with the cleanout holes drilled, tapped and plugs installed.

19- Inside view of the centrifuge cup with rings welded in place. Ugly but should work. A bit of silicone to help seal up the upper ring should help a bit.

20- The 48" centrifuge that 200 or more tons per hour flow through. The tub under the pipe is where the concentrates flush out.

21- The 7.5" centrifuge I used to reconcentrate the concentrates from the 48" unit.

22- Another view showing the catch sluice and tails bucket.

23- What the rubber mat in the head of the catch sluice looks like when the centrifuge starts puking gold.

24- The sluice riffles when the centrifuge is puking gold. Might be 4-6 ounces in the box and the tails are still full of gold too. Dump the sluice in the tails bucket and rerun it all.

25- The centrifuge cup plugged up with gold. Likely well over a troy pound of gold here.

26- Panning a pound or two of gold from the 7.5" concentrator.

27- Magnetics removed, barite washed out and gold clean enough to melt. Likely 70 percent gold at this time.

28- Nuggets screened out, time to pick out trash. The cleaner you get it in the previous step, the easier this step is.

29- A quart mason jar full of gold. How cool is that.